Animal World

Sharks

Donna Bailey

RSVP
RAINTREE
STECK-VAUGHN
PUBLISHERS

Did you know that a shark's skeleton is not
made of bones?
Shark skeletons are made of
tough, white gristle called cartilage.
Humans have cartilage in their ears.

2

A shark's tough, leathery skin protects
it from attacks by other creatures.
Little fish called remora eat tiny parasites that
grow on the shark's skin.
Remora use suckers on their heads to attach
themselves to the shark.

Sharks are good swimmers.
But, unlike other fish, sharks cannot
move their fins or use them as brakes.
Sharks cannot swim backward or stop.

Sharks have a keen sense of smell
which they use when hunting for food.
A shark can smell blood in the water
more than a mile away.
Blood in the water attracts hungry sharks.

Sharks also hear very well.
A shark has a line of sensors
along each side of its body.
The shark can sense small movements
of water made by a school of fish.

6

Once a shark has found its prey,
it relies on its sight for the last
moments of the hunt.
The shark circles its victim, then makes
a high-speed run directly toward it.

If the prey is small, the shark
simply snaps it up in its powerful jaws.
It bites off the flesh of larger prey.
Sharks get excited by the smell of blood.
A shark will return again and
again to tear its victim apart.

Sharks sometimes hunt in a mob with
other sharks.
The mob can get so excited by the smell of
blood that the sharks attack in a frenzy.

Sharks in a frenzy become very excited
as they circle around rapidly.
As the frenzy increases, the sharks
begin to bite anything within range.
The sharks even attack each other.

The jaws of a hunting shark are
under its snout.
Dozens of sharp teeth are set in rows in the
shark's powerful jaws.
But sharks use only one row at a time.
The other teeth lie flat against the back
of the jaw, protected by a flap of flesh.

Sharks' teeth are only loosely fixed
to their jaws and often get torn loose
during an attack.
Fresh teeth from the second row replace
the teeth that are lost.

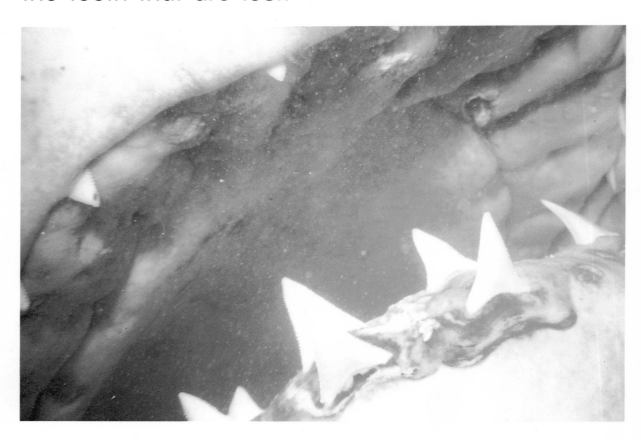

When a shark bites its prey, the shark tilts
its snout up out of the way.
Its jaws swing down and forward
so that the shark's mouth opens at
the front of its body.

Many sharks swim with their mouth open.
Water enters its mouth and the shark takes in
oxygen as the water passes over its gills.
The shark opens the gills on each side of
its head to push the water out.

If a shark stops swimming for a long time,
no water flows over its gills.
The shark will suffocate from lack of oxygen.
This is why most sharks never sleep or
rest, but swim all the time.

A nurse shark does not need to swim
to breathe.
It gets oxygen by pumping water over its gills
as it lies on the ocean floor.

A nurse shark prefers to lie very still
on the ocean floor.
There, the nurse shark waits for crabs and
fish to come within range of its jaws.
If it is disturbed by people who are swimming,
a nurse shark will attack.

There are over 300 kinds of sharks.

They live in most of the oceans of the world.

The largest shark, the whale shark, may reach
a length of 50 feet and weigh several tons!

The whale shark is quite harmless.

It feeds on tiny animals called krill, which it filters
out of the water as it swims.

18

Most people think sharks are dangerous
creatures that attack and kill people.
In fact, there are only about 30 kinds of
dangerous sharks.
The most dangerous is the
great white shark.

Divers wear special shark suits in
waters where they know
great white sharks can be found.

A great white shark may even try to
attack a diver in a diving cage.
It will bite the bars of the cage
as it tries to get at the diver.

Sharks swim far and fast.

They roam the ocean and hunt

the schools of fish on the surface.

The mako shark is probably the fastest.

It can swim as fast as 60 miles an hour.

22

Some sharks, such as the great white shark, prefer to travel and hunt alone.
Others hunt together in a mob, like these whitetip reef sharks.

Blue sharks roam the oceans, and
travel hundreds of miles between
their summer and winter feeding grounds.
They follow schools of fish and squid.
This blue shark is feeding on squid.

This shark is called a great hammerhead.

Its head is T-shaped like a hammer.

Its eyes and nostrils are in each end
of the hammer.

The great hammerhead swims both in shallow
coastal waters and in the ocean depths.

A tiger shark has unusual markings.
When it is young, the shark has a pattern of
spots on its back like those of a leopard.
The tiger shark swims in shallow water.

As a tiger shark gets older, the markings
on its back change into stripes.
That is how the tiger shark got its name.
Later the marks disappear.

The swell shark is speckled so that
it can hide among the stones at
the bottom of shallow waters.

28

Most sharks give birth to live young.
But a few kinds of sharks lay eggs.
The baby shark grows from an embryo
inside a tough, leathery egg case.
This swell shark embryo is one month old.

At three months, the embryo has grown
eyes and a tail.
The shark embryo has a yolk sac which
feeds the growing shark.

30

Sometime between eight and ten months, the
baby swell shark hatches from the egg.
The hatchling has a double row of
big, spiky teeth on its back to help it
cut its way through the egg case.
At first, it still gets food from the yolk sac.

The young swell shark soon begins to hunt
for food.
Baby sharks must take care of themselves
because mother sharks do not feed them.

Index

biting 8, 10, 13
blood 5, 8, 9
blue sharks 24
breathing 14, 15, 16
cartilage 2
divers 20, 21
eggs 29, 31
embryo 29, 30
fins 4
food 17, 18, 22, 24, 32
frenzy 9, 10
gills 14, 15, 16
great hammerhead shark 25
great white shark 19, 20, 21, 23
hearing 6
hunting 5, 7, 9, 23

jaws 8, 11, 12, 13
mako shark 22
mob 9, 23
mouth 13, 14
nurse shark 16, 17
remora 3
skeleton 2
skin 3
sleeping 15
smelling 5
swell shark 28, 29, 30, 31, 32
swimming 4, 15
teeth 11, 12, 31
tiger shark 26, 27
whale shark 18
whitetip reef sharks 23
yolk sac 30, 31

Editorial Consultant: Donna Bailey
Executive Editor: Elizabeth Strauss
Project Editor: Becky Ward

Picture research by Jennifer Garratt
Designed by Richard Garratt Design

Photographs
Cover: Planet Earth Pictures (Herwarth Voigtmann)
Ardea London Limited: title page, 5, 6, 8, 10, 11, 15, 23 (Ron & Valerie Taylor)
OSF Picture Library: 3 (J. Barnett); 12 (Kim Westerkov); 17 (J. E. Paling)
Planet Earth Pictures: 2, 7, 18, 19, 20, 21, 22, 24 (Marty Snyderman); 4 (Kurt Amsler); 9 (Mark Conlin); 14 (Doug Perrine); 16, 27, 28 (Kenneth Lucas); 29, 30, 31, 32 (A. Kerstich); 25 (Warren Williams)
Seaphot Limited: 13 (Herwarth Voigtmann); 26 (Christian Petron)

Library of Congress Cataloging-in-Publication Data: Bailey, Donna.   Sharks / Donna Bailey.   p.   cm.—(Animal world)   Includes index.   SUMMARY: Studies the physical characteristics, behavior, and life cycle of different kinds of sharks.   ISBN 0-8114-2649-1   1. Sharks—Juvenile literature. [1. Sharks.]   I. Title.   II. Series: Animal world (Austin, Tex.)   QL638.9.B33   1991   597′.31—dc20   90-22114   CIP   AC